FOOD LOVERS

CHICKEN

FOOD LOVERS

CHICKEN

RECIPES SELECTED BY JONNIE LÉGER

Trans
Atlantic
Press

All recipes serve four people, unless otherwise indicated.

CONTENTS

POT AU FEU

Ingredients

8 scallions (spring onions)

9 oz / 250 g asparagus

1 garlic clove

4 tbsp olive oil

1 chicken, cut into 8 pieces

1 tbsp thyme

2 bay leaves

 $^2/_3$ cup / 200 ml chicken broth (stock)

1 lb / 450 g small potatoes

7 oz / 200 g small carrots

Salt and pepper

Method

Prep and cook time: 1 hour

1 Cut the scallions (spring onions) and asparagus into short lengths. Finely chop the garlic.

2 Heat the oil in a large skillet (frying pan), add the chicken pieces and fry until browned on all sides.

3 Add the garlic, thyme and bay leaves to the chicken, stir briefly, then add the broth (stock). Simmer gently for 30 minutes.

4 Add the scallions, asparagus, potatoes and carrots and simmer for a further 20 minutes until the vegetables are tender. Season to taste with salt and pepper before serving.

CHICKEN CACCIATORE

Ingredients

1 onion

1 garlic clove

1 lb 8 oz / 650 g boneless chicken thighs, skinned

1 tbsp olive oil

1 tsp chopped fresh oregano, plus extra to garnish

½ tsp celery salt

Salt and pepper

7 tbsp white wine

14 oz / 400 g can chopped tomatoes

½ tsp sugar

12 oz / 350 g tagliatelle

Black olives, to garnish

Method

Prep and cook time: 50 min

1 Finely chop the onion and crush the garlic. Cut the chicken into chunks. Heat the oil in a skillet (frying pan), add the onions, garlic and oregano and fry for about 3 minutes, until softened.

2 Add the chicken pieces, sprinkle in the celery salt and season with pepper. Cook for 10 minutes, turning occasionally, until lightly browned.

3 Pour in the wine and bring to a simmer. Add the tomatoes and sugar, cover with a lid and leave to simmer for 20 minutes until the chicken is tender and cooked through.

4 Meanwhile, bring a large saucepan of salted water to the boil. Add the tagliatelle and cook according to the packet instructions. Drain well.

5 Serve the chicken garnished with black olives and oregano and accompany with the pasta.

CHICKEN AND HAM PIE

Ingredients

1 lb / 450 g boneless chicken breasts, skinned

1¼ cups / 300 ml chicken broth (stock)

8 oz / 225 g cooked ham

1 shallot

4 tbsp / 50 g butter

2 tbsp all-purpose (plain) flour

⅔ cup / 150 g crème fraîche

2 tbsp lemon juice

2 egg yolks

3 tbsp grated Cheddar cheese

2 tbsp finely chopped fresh parsley

Freshly grated nutmeg

Salt and pepper

For the pastry:

2 cups / 200 g all-purpose (plain) flour

1 tsp salt

5 tbsp / 70 g cold butter

5 tbsp / 70 g shortening or lard

1–2 tbsp ice-cold water

Flour, for dusting

Method

Prep and cook time: 1 hour 40 min

1 To make the pastry, put the flour and salt into a large bowl. Add the butter and shortening or lard, in small pieces, and rub in with your fingertips until the mixture forms breadcrumbs. Add enough ice-cold water to form a dough. Wrap in plastic wrap (cling film) and put into the refrigerator while you make the filling.

2 Preheat the oven to 200°C (400°F / Gas Mark 6). Cut the chicken into small, bite-size cubes. Put the broth (stock) into a saucepan and bring to the boil. Add the chicken and cook for 4–5 minutes. Remove from the pan with a slotted spoon, reserving the broth.

3 Cut the ham into small cubes, discarding any fat. Finely chop the shallot. Melt 1 tbsp / 15 g butter in a saucepan. Add the shallot and fry until translucent. Add the ham and fry for about 3 minutes then remove from the heat.

4 Heat the remaining butter in a separate pan. Add the flour and stir until it has absorbed the fat. Gradually stir in the broth, bring to the boil, stirring, and then remove from the heat.

5 Put the crème fraîche, lemon juice and 1 egg yolk in a bowl and mix together. Stir into the sauce with the cheese. Add the chicken, ham and parsley and mix well together. Season with nutmeg, salt and pepper.

6 Divide the pastry in half and roll out each half on a floured surface into a round large enough to fit a 9 inch (23 cm) ovenproof pie dish.

7 Put 1 round in the base of the dish and add the chicken filling. Place the second round on top and press the edges together to seal.

8 Beat the remaining egg yolk and brush on top to glaze. Bake in the oven for about 40 minutes until golden brown.

TANDOORI CHICKEN KEBABS

Ingredients

4 boneless chicken breasts, skinned

Salt and pepper

Juice of 1 lemon

2 garlic cloves

1 walnut-sized piece fresh ginger

1 cup / 200 g plain yogurt

2 tbsp vegetable oil

¼ tsp ground cumin

¼ tsp ground nutmeg

¼ tsp ground coriander

¼ tsp black pepper

¼ tsp paprika

For the raita:

1 cucumber

1¼ cups / 250 g plain yogurt

1 tbsp finely chopped fresh parsley

1 tbsp finely chopped fresh mint

½ tsp ground caraway

½ tsp ground coriander

Salt and pepper

Mint leaves, to garnish

Method

Prep and cook time: 40 min plus 12 hours marinating and 1 hour standing time for the raita

1 Cut the chicken into bite-size pieces and put in a shallow dish. Season with salt and pepper and drizzle over the lemon juice.

2 To make the marinade, crush the garlic. Peel and grate the ginger. Put in a bowl, add the yogurt, oil and the spices, and mix together.

3 Generously brush the chicken with the marinade and cover the dish with foil. Leave to marinate in the refrigerator overnight.

4 To make the raita, peel, remove the seeds from and grate the cucumber. Put in a bowl, add the yogurt, parsley, mint, caraway and coriander, and season to taste with salt and pepper. Leave to stand for 1 hour.

5 Preheat the broiler (grill) and cover the rack with foil. Skewer the chicken pieces on to kebab sticks, reserving the marinade.

6 Cook the kebabs for about 8–10 minutes, turning halfway through the cooking time and brushing with the reserved marinade.

7 Serve the tandoori chicken kebabs with the raita, garnished with mint leaves.

SPINACH AND CHICKEN SALAD

Ingredients

2 boneless chicken breasts, skinned

2 tbsp light soy sauce

2 nori seaweed leaves

4 oz / 120 g cooked ham

1 red bell pepper

1 lb / 450 g fresh baby spinach

4 tbsp sesame oil

2 tbsp rice wine vinegar

Salt and pepper

2 tbsp sunflower oil

2 tbsp sesame seeds

Method

Prep and cook time: 35 min plus 20 min marinating

1 Cut the chicken breasts into bite-size pieces and put in a bowl. Add the soy sauce and leave to marinate for 20 minutes.

2 Meanwhile, slice the nori leaves and ham into thin strips. Core and finely slice the red pepper, discarding the core and seeds.

3 Rinse the spinach and shake to remove excess water.

4 To make the dressing, put the sesame oil rice wine vinegar, salt and pepper in a jug and whisk together.

5 Heat the sunflower oil in a skillet (frying pan), add the chicken pieces and fry until golden brown all over and cooked through.

6 Mix the spinach with the red pepper and toss in the dressing. Add more seasoning if wished. Carefully toss the chicken with the spinach.

7 Arrange the salad on serving plates. Garnish with the ham and nori strips and sprinkle the sesame seeds on top. Serve at once.

JAMBALAYA

Ingredients

4 boneless chicken breasts, skinned

1 onion

1 celery stalk

2 garlic cloves

3 scallions (spring onions)

2 red bell peppers

2 red chilies

3 tbsp olive oil

1¼ cups / 250 g long grain rice

2 cups / 475 ml chicken broth (stock)

1 bay leaf

Salt and pepper

¾ cup / 150 g canned chopped tomatoes

2 tbsp chopped fresh cilantro (coriander) leaves

Ground cumin

Method

Prep and cook time: 50 min

1 Cut the chicken into slices. Chop the onion, celery and garlic. Slice the scallions (spring onions) into rings. Finely slice the red peppers and chilies, discarding the cores and seeds.

2 Heat the oil in a large skillet (frying pan), add the onion, garlic and scallions and fry for 2–3 minutes. Add the chicken and continue to fry for 1–2 minutes.

3 Stir in the celery, red pepper, chilies and rice. Pour in the chicken broth (stock) and add the bay leaf. Season with salt and pepper.

4 Cover the pan and simmer for about 20 minutes, stirring occasionally. When the rice is cooked, add the tomatoes and cilantro (coriander) leaves. Before serving, season to taste with cumin, salt and pepper.

CHICKEN SALTIMBOCCA

Ingredients

3 tbsp olive oil, plus extra to grease

4 boneless chicken breasts, skinned

7 oz / 200 g mozzarella cheese

8 slices prosciutto

8 sage leaves

Salt and pepper

7 tbsp dry white wine

Small bunch watercress, to garnish

Method
Prep and cook time: 35 min

1 Preheat the oven to 200°C (400°F / Gas Mark 6). Lightly oil a roasting pan.

2 Slice each chicken breast in half horizontally. Beat with a meat mallet or wooden rolling pin to flatten slightly.

3 Heat 2 tbsp oil in a large skillet (frying pan) and briefly brown the chicken pieces on both sides. Remove from the pan and place in the prepared roasting pan.

4 Slice the mozzarella cheese. Put a prosciutto slice, a sage leaf and 2 slices of mozzarella cheese on each chicken breast. Season lightly with salt and pepper.

5 Cook in the oven for about 8 minutes until golden brown.

6 Remove the chicken pieces from the roasting pan once they are cooked through. Add the wine to the pan and cook on the hob, stirring all the time to deglaze the pan, until the sauce has reduced slightly.

7 Serve the saltimbocca with the sauce poured over the top and garnish with the watercress.

STICKY HONEY AND MUSTARD CHICKEN WINGS

Ingredients

4 tbsp thick honey

4 tbsp Dijon mustard

4 tbsp olive oil

1 tsp mustard seeds (optional)

Grated zest and juice of 2 lemons

12 chicken wings

Salt and pepper

1 scallion (spring onion), to garnish

Method
Prep and cook time: 1 hour

1 Put the honey, mustard, olive oil, mustard seeds, if using, the lemon zest and juice in a bowl and mix together.

2 Put the chicken wings into a large, non-metallic ovenproof dish and season with salt and pepper.

3 Drizzle over the honey and mustard mixture and stir to mix into the chicken wings. Cover and leave to marinate in the refrigerator for about 20 minutes.

4 Meanwhile, preheat the oven to 200°C (400°F / Gas Mark 6). Roast the chicken wings, basting occasionally, for 20–30 minutes until golden brown and thoroughly cooked through.

5 Meanwhile, shred the scallion (spring onion) and put into a bowl of cold water. Chill in the refrigerator to make the scallions curl.

6 Serve the chicken wings garnished with the scallion curls.

CHICKEN BREASTS IN COCONUT MILK

Ingredients

1 carrot

1 leek

2 celery stalks

1 bay leaf

1 red chili

2 boneless chicken breasts, with skin on

1 tbsp / 15 g butter

1 tbsp sugar

2 tsp finely chopped fresh ginger

1 cup / 225 ml coconut milk

Salt and pepper

6 oz / 150 g corn salad (lamb's lettuce)

3 tbsp olive oil

2 tbsp balsamic vinegar

1 cup / 35 g basil leaves

Method

Prep and cook time: 45 min

1 Roughly chop the carrot, leek and celery and put in a wide saucepan. Add the bay leaf. Finely chop the chili, discarding the seeds, and set aside.

2 Lay the chicken breasts on top of the vegetables, add enough water just to cover the meat and bring to a gentle boil. Simmer for about 15 minutes and remove from the heat.

3 Melt the butter and sugar in a clean pan over high heat and allow to caramelize slightly. As soon as the sugar starts to caramelize add the chopped chili and ginger. Pour in the coconut milk and cook until reduced slightly. Season with salt and pepper.

5 Arrange the corn salad (lamb's lettuce) on a serving dish. Dress with the olive oil and balsamic.

6 Coarsely chop the basil leaves and add to the coconut milk sauce.

7 Remove the chicken breasts from the pan and slice. Add to the serving plates and drizzle over the sauce to serve.

CHICKEN AND ASPARAGUS RISOTTO

Ingredients

1 lb / 450 g asparagus

1 garlic clove

5 tbsp olive oil

4 boneless chicken breasts, skinned

Salt and pepper

¾ cup / 150 g risotto rice

2 cups / 475 ml vegetable broth (stock)

1 tbsp / 15 g butter

½ cup / 50 g freshly grated Parmesan cheese

1 tbsp fresh thyme leaves

Method

Prep and cook time: 55 min

1 Peel the bottom third from the asparagus stalks and cut the spears into bite-size pieces. Crush the garlic.

2 Heat 2 tbsp oil in a large skillet (frying pan), add the garlic and fry for 30 seconds. Add the asparagus, fry for 1–2 minutes, then add a little water and cook very gently until tender but still with a slight bite. Remove from the skillet and set aside.

3 Cut the chicken breasts into dice. Heat 2 tbsp oil in the skillet, add the chicken pieces and fry until browned on all sides and cooked through. Season with salt and pepper and remove from the pan.

4 Heat the remaining 1 tbsp oil in the pan. Add the rice and stir until slightly translucent, then add a ladleful of broth (stock) and stir until it has been absorbed. Continue in this way, gradually adding more broth and stirring all the time, until the rice is tender but still has a slight bite and the risotto is creamy. This will take about 20 minutes.

5 Stir in the chicken and asparagus and add the butter and grated Parmesan cheese. Season to taste with salt and pepper, stir in the thyme leaves and serve.

CARIBBEAN COCONUT CHICKEN

Ingredients

4 boneless chicken breasts, skinned

1 onion

1 garlic clove

1 red bell pepper

1 green bell pepper

2 tbsp sunflower oil

¾ cup / 60 g grated coconut

Grated zest and juice of 1 lime

½ tsp paprika

½ tsp red chili paste

1 tsp salt

1 tbsp / 15 g butter

1 tsp apricot jam

Method

Prep and cook time: 1 hour

1 Preheat the oven to 190°C (375°F / Gas Mark 5). Put the chicken breasts between 2 sheets of plastic wrap (cling film) and, using a mallet or wooden rolling pin, beat the meat until flattened.

2 Finely chop the onion and garlic. Finely chop the red and green pepper, discarding the cores and seeds.

3 Heat the oil in a skillet (frying pan). Add the onion and garlic and fry over a medium heat for 2–3 minutes. Add the peppers and fry until softened. Stir in the coconut and remove the pan from the heat. Stir in the lime zest.

4 Place an equal amount of the vegetables in the centre of each chicken breast. Fold the ends over the top of the filling and secure with toothpicks (cocktail sticks).

5 Put the paprika, chili paste and salt in a small bowl and mix together. Brush each chicken roll with the marinade.

6 Melt the butter in a roasting pan, add the chicken rolls and bake in the oven for 25–30 minutes until golden brown, basting from time to time.

7 Remove the chicken from the pan and keep warm. Stir the apricot jam and lime juice into the pan juices. Bring to a boil, reduce the heat, and simmer for 2–3 minutes, stirring all the time. Serve the chicken with the sauce poured over the top.

ROAST LEMON CHICKEN

Ingredients

3 lemons

2 tbsp vegetable oil

Salt and pepper

1 large chicken

2 lb / 900 g small waxy potatoes

8 sprigs thyme

2 cups / 475 ml chicken broth (stock)

4 scallions (spring onions)

1 red bell pepper

1 tbsp honey

4 tsp sherry

Method

Prep and cook time: 1 hour 40 min

1 Preheat the oven to 190°C (375°F / Gas Mark 5). Remove the zest from 1 lemon and slice all the lemons.

2 Mix half the lemon zest with 1 tbsp oil and salt and pepper. Rub the mixture all over the chicken. Tie the legs together with string and tuck the wings under the chicken.

3 Peel the potatoes and put in a roasting pan with the lemon slices. Place the chicken, breast side down, in the pan and add the thyme sprigs.

4 Roast in the oven for 30 minutes, occasionally pouring some of the chicken broth (stock) over the top and basting with the pan juices.

5 Meanwhile, cut the scallions (spring onions) into short lengths. Roughly chop the red pepper, discarding the core and seeds.

6 Remove the chicken from the pan and add the scallions and red pepper to the roasting pan.

7 Put the honey, sherry, remaining oil and lemon zest in a bowl and mix together. Return the chicken to the pan, breast side up, baste with the marinade and sprinkle with salt and pepper.

8 Roast the chicken for a further 35–45 minutes until golden brown. Check that the juices run clear. To serve, arrange the roast chicken, lemon slices and vegetables on a serving platter. Season the pan juices to taste and serve as a sauce.

SPICY POUSSIN

Ingredients

4 poussins, each weighing about
1 lb / 450 g, or 2 spring chickens

Sea salt

4 garlic cloves

1 tbsp dried oregano

2 tsp paprika

1 tsp coarsely ground black pepper

Grated zest and juice of 2 lemons

4 tbsp olive oil

1¼ cups / 300 ml chicken
broth (stock)

2 tbsp balsamic vinegar

2 roasted red bell peppers

4 handfuls wild arugula (rocket)

½ cup / 50 g Parmesan cheese

8 tsp chili jam, to garnish

Method

Prep and cook time: 1 hour

1 Preheat the oven to 200°C (400°F / Gas Mark 6).
Put the poussins in a large roasting pan and season
with sea salt.

2 Crush the garlic and sprinkle over the poussins
with the oregano, paprika, black pepper and lemon
zest. Drizzle over the lemon juice and olive oil.

3 Add the chicken broth (stock) and balsamic
vinegar to the roasting pan, cover with foil and roast
for 20 minutes (or 35 minutes for spring chicken).

4 Remove the foil, baste the birds with the juices
and roast for a further 15 minutes until the birds
are browned and thoroughly cooked through.

5 Meanwhile, cut the red peppers into quarters,
discarding the cores and seeds.

6 Place the poussins on serving plates with some
of the pan juices, each with 2 pepper quarters and a
handful of arugula (rocket).

7 Using a vegetable peeler, shave the Parmesan
cheese on top. Season with black pepper and serve
garnished with chili jam.

CHICKEN AND PUMPKIN PATTIES

Ingredients

1 lb / 450 g pumpkin

6 shallots

4 tbsp olive oil

3 tsp garam masala

1 lb / 450 g ground (minced) chicken

3 cups / 150 g wholemeal breadcrumbs

1 cup / 25 g chopped fresh parsley

2 eggs

3–4 tbsp all-purpose (plain) flour

Salt and pepper

Mango wedges, to garnish

Method

Prep and cook time: 40 min

1 Peel the pumpkin and discard the seeds. Coarsely grate the flesh and put in a large bowl. Finely chop the shallots.

2 Heat 1 tbsp of the oil in a skillet (frying pan) and gently fry the shallots until translucent.

3 Add the garam masala and cook for 2 minutes, then remove from the heat and leave to cool.

4 Add the chicken, breadcrumbs, parsley, eggs, 2 tbsp of the flour and the cooled shallots to the pumpkin and mix together. Season with salt and pepper.

5 Put the remaining flour on to a large plate. Form the chicken mixture into 16–20 patties and lightly coat each one in the flour.

6 Heat the remaining oil in a skillet and fry the patties for 4 minutes on each side, ensuring the chicken is cooked through. Serve garnished with mango wedges.

CHICKEN WITH FORTY CLOVES OF GARLIC

Ingredients

1 red onion

40 garlic cloves

1 lemon

4 chicken breasts, on the bone
and skinned

Salt and pepper

5 tbsp olive oil

6 sprigs thyme

4 bay leaves

½ cup / 125 ml water

Method

Prep and cook time: 1 hour 50 min

1 Preheat the oven to 200°C (400°F / Gas Mark 6).
Cut the onion into wedges and skin the garlic
cloves. Slice the lemon.

2 Generously season the chicken with salt
and pepper.

3 Heat the oil in a large flameproof casserole. Add
the chicken and onion and cook for 10 minutes,
turning occasionally, until the chicken is browned
on all sides.

4 Add the thyme, 2 bay leaves, lemon slices and
garlic cloves, baste with the oil and meat juices and
pour in the water.

5 Cover with a tight fitting lid and cook in the oven
for 1½ hours until the chicken and garlic are very
tender. Serve garnished with the remaining bay leaves.

CHICKEN WITH RICOTTA STUFFING

Ingredients

1 lb 12 oz / 800 g small new potatoes

4 garlic cloves

½ cup / 125 ml olive oil

5 oz / 150 g ricotta cheese

Salt and pepper

4 boneless chicken thighs,
with skin on

1 lb / 450 g string (runner) beans

3 scallions (spring onions)

4 tbsp / 50 g butter

4 tbsp chopped fresh parsley

Method

Prep and cook time: 1 hour 20 min

1 Preheat the oven to 190°C (375°F / Gas Mark 5).
Cook the potatoes in a saucepan of boiling salted water
for 20–25 minutes until tender. Drain well.

2 Finely chop the garlic and put in a bowl. Add 2 tbsp
oil and the ricotta cheese. Season with salt and pepper
and mix together.

3 Loosen the skin on the chicken thighs by running your
fingers between the skin and the meat. Spoon the ricotta
mixture under the skin, dividing it equally among the
thighs. Season with salt and pepper.

4 Heat 2 tbsp of the oil in a roasting pan. Add the
chicken thighs and sear on all sides. Roast in the oven
for about 30 minutes, basting from time to time.

5 Cut the potatoes into wedges and place in a lightly
greased casserole dish. Brush with the remaining oil and
sprinkle with pepper. Bake in the oven for 10 minutes
until you can pierce the potatoes easily with a fork.

6 Meanwhile, cook the beans in salted boiling water
for about 10 minutes until tender. Drain well.

7 Finely chop the scallions (spring onions). Melt the
butter in a saucepan, add the scallions and fry for
4–5 minutes. Stir in the chopped parsley. Season with
salt and pepper.

8 Arrange the potatoes, beans and chicken thighs on
the serving plates and serve with the scallions spooned
over the top.

CHICKEN BALLS

Ingredients

3 slices day-old white bread

Generous ¾ cup / 200 ml whipping cream

1 tbsp chopped scallions (spring onions), plus extra to garnish

1 lb 8 oz / 650 g ground (minced) chicken

3 tbsp lemon juice

2 tbsp chopped fresh lemon balm or lemon thyme

2 tbsp chopped fresh mint

Salt and pepper

6 tbsp fresh breadcrumbs

2 tbsp sesame seeds

4 tbsp vegetable oil

Carrot ribbons, to garnish

Method

Prep and cook time: 30 min

1 Tear the bread into small pieces and put in a large bowl. Add the cream and leave until softened.

2 Finely chop the scallions (spring onions). Add to the bread with the chicken, lemon juice, lemon balm or thyme and the mint, and mix together. Season with salt and pepper.

3 With damp hands, form the meat mixture into balls. You should make about 20.

4 Put the breadcrumbs and sesame seeds in a shallow dish and mix together. Coat the chicken balls in the mixture.

5 Heat the oil in a skillet (frying pan), add the chicken balls and fry for about 5 minutes, browning all sides until thoroughly cooked through. Serve garnished with the scallions and carrot ribbons.

CHICKEN BREASTS ON A BED OF VEGETABLES

Ingredients

1 lb / 450 g asparagus

1 lb / 450 g string (runner) beans

12 oz / 350 g snow (sugar snap) peas

4 boneless chicken breasts, skinned

Salt and pepper

6 tbsp / 75 g butter

4 tbsp lemon juice

4 tbsp small capers

Grated lemon zest, to garnish

Method

Prep and cook time: 40 min

1 Peel the bottom third from the asparagus stalks and trim the ends. Top and tail the beans.

2 Put the asparagus and beans in a saucepan of boiling salted water and simmer for about 6 minutes.

3 Add the snow (sugar snap) peas to the pan and continue simmering for a further 4 minutes. Drain well, immerse the vegetables in cold water and drain again. Return to the pan.

4 Season the chicken breasts with salt and pepper. Heat 2 tbsp (25 g) butter in a skillet (frying pan) until melted. Add the chicken breasts and fry for about 5 minutes on each side until cooked through.

5 Add the remaining 4 tbsp (50 g) butter to the vegetables and heat until melted and the vegetables are hot. Add the lemon juice and season with the salt and pepper.

6 To serve, divide the vegetables and butter sauce between 4 serving plates. Put a chicken breast on top of each and sprinkle with the capers and lemon zest to garnish.

CHICKEN, AVOCADO AND STRAWBERRY SALAD

Ingredients

Half an iceberg lettuce

8 oz / 225 g strawberries

1 cup / 100 g seedless grapes

1 avocado

4 boneless chicken breasts, skinned

½ tbsp / 10 g butter

1 tsp curry powder

1 tsp dried thyme

Salt and pepper

For the dressing:

3 tbsp white wine vinegar

1 tbsp lemon juice

3 tbsp sunflower oil

1 tbsp rapeseed oil

Salt and pepper

Method

Prep and cook time: 30 min

1 To make the dressing, put the vinegar, lemon juice, sunflower and rapeseed oil in a large bowl and mix together. Season with salt and pepper.

2 Tear the lettuce leaves into bite-size pieces and arrange on serving plates. Hull and slice the strawberries. Halve the grapes. Slice the avocado in half lengthways and slice the flesh.

3 Add the avocado and strawberries to the dressing and carefully mix together. Add the grapes.

4 Slice the chicken into strips. Heat the butter in a skillet (frying pan), add the chicken slices and fry gently for about 5 minutes until lightly browned on all sides and cooked through.

5 Add the curry powder and thyme and season with salt and pepper. Cook gently for a further 4–5 minutes until the chicken is tender.

6 Arrange the meat on top of the lettuce. Pour the dressed avocado and strawberries on top and serve at once.

CHICKEN BREAST STUFFED WITH TOMATO

Ingredients

4 oz / 120 g dried tomatoes in oil

4 tbsp chopped fresh basil

3 tbsp grated Parmesan cheese

1 tbsp toasted pine nuts

3 tbsp olive oil

Salt and pepper

2 large red bell peppers

1 tbsp vegetable oil, for greasing

4 boneless chicken breasts, skinned

1 tbsp lemon juice

8 slices bacon

Method

Prep and cook time: 50 min

1 Preheat the oven to 190°C (375°F / Gas Mark 5). Drain the tomatoes and finely chop.

2 To make the pesto, put the basil, Parmesan cheese, pine nuts and olive oil in a food processor and blend together to form a purée. Season with salt and pepper.

3 Remove the stems, cores and seeds from the peppers and cut into quarters. Place, skin side up, in a lightly greased ovenproof dish. Brush a little oil on the peppers.

4 Make a horizontal cut along each chicken breast to form a pocket. Rub each breast, inside and out, with the lemon juice, salt and pepper. Fill the pockets with the tomatoes and pesto.

5 Wrap each chicken breast with two strips of bacon and put in the prepared dish with the peppers.

6 Bake in the oven for about 25 minutes, until tender and cooked through.

CHICKEN CAESAR SALAD

Ingredients

4 garlic cloves

2 egg yolks

2 anchovy fillets

2 tbsp lemon juice

Salt and pepper

8 tbsp olive oil

2 tbsp chopped fresh parsley

½ cup / 50 g grated
Parmesan cheese

2 boneless chicken breasts, skinned

2 tbsp vegetable oil

3 slices day-old white bread

½ cup / 120 g butter

1 romaine (cos) lettuce

Method

Prep and cook time: 45 min

1 For the dressing, crush 3 garlic cloves and put in a bowl with the egg yolks.

2 Rinse the anchovies in cool water and chop finely. Add to the egg yolks with the lemon juice, salt and pepper. Beat until creamy.

3 Sir in the oil, drop by drop, until the dressing thickens.

4 Add the parsley and cheese and mix together. Set aside.

5 Season the chicken with salt and pepper. Heat the oil in a skillet (frying pan) and fry the chicken for about 5 minutes on each side or until cooked through. Remove the chicken from the skillet and set aside.

6 Cut the bread into small cubes. Wipe the skillet with paper towels and rub the remaining garlic clove over base. Add the butter and fry the bread cubes until crunchy. Remove the cubes from the pan.

7 Tear the lettuce leaves into bite-size pieces and toss together with the dressing. Slice the chicken diagonally into slices and serve alongside the salad. Sprinkle the bread croûtons on top to garnish.

PAD THAI

Ingredients

8 oz / 225 g rice noodles

2 boneless chicken breasts, skinned

2 tbsp soy sauce

2–3 tbsp oyster sauce

1 onion

3 garlic cloves

1 red chili

2 scallions (spring onions)

1 lime

5 oz / 150 g unsalted cashew nuts

3 tbsp vegetable oil

Salt and pepper

8 oz / 225 g peeled shrimps (prawns)

2/3 cup / 150 ml chicken broth (stock)

4 sprigs fresh cilantro (coriander),
to garnish

Method

Prep and cook time: 45 min

1 Cook the noodles according to the packet instructions. Rinse under cold water and drain well.

2 Meanwhile, slice the chicken breasts into strips. Put in a large bowl, add the soy and oyster sauces and leave to marinate for a few minutes.

3 Chop the onion and finely chop the garlic. Finely chop the chili, discarding the seeds. Finely chop the white parts of the scallions (spring onions) and slice the green parts on the diagonal into rings. Cut the lime into 8 wedges. Roughly chop the cashew nuts.

4 Heat the oil in a wok. Add the chicken slices, reserving the marinade, and sear quickly. Remove from the wok and season with salt.

5 Add the onions, garlic and chili to the remaining oil in the wok. Add the shrimps (prawns) and fry briefly. Pour in the broth (stock) and simmer for 2 minutes.

6 Mix the noodles, chicken and reserved marinade together. Season with salt and pepper. Add the scallions and mix together.

7 Turn the mixture into the wok and heat through. Serve sprinkled with the cashew nuts, garnished with cilantro (coriander) sprigs and accompanied with the lime wedges.

CREAMY CHICKEN WITH LEEKS

Ingredients

1 onion

4 baby leeks

4 boneless chicken breasts, skinned

2 tbsp olive oil

Salt and pepper

1 tbsp all-purpose (plain) flour

1 cup / 200 g long grain rice

1¼ cups / 300 ml chicken broth (stock)

¾ cup / 200 ml crème fraîche

2 tbsp chopped fresh tarragon

Lime wedges, to garnish

Method

Prep and cook time: 50 min

1 Chop the onion. Slice the leeks into shreds. Cut the chicken into thick slices.

2 Heat the oil in a large skillet (frying pan) and add the onion and leeks. Cook gently for 2 minutes, then remove 1 tbsp of the lightly cooked leeks and set aside to garnish.

3 Add the chicken to the pan, season generously with salt and pepper and cook for 5 minutes until browned on all sides.

4 Sprinkle over the flour and cook for 1 minute, then gradually stir in the broth (stock). Cover the pan and simmer for 15 minutes.

5 Cook the rice according to the packet instructions. Drain well.

6 Stir the crème fraîche and tarragon into the chicken and heat through for 2–3 minutes. Check that the chicken is thoroughly cooked through. Serve the chicken on top of the rice and garnish with the reserved leeks and a lime wedge.

MOROCCAN CHICKEN WITH PUMPKIN

Ingredients

1 lb / 450 g pumpkin

1 lb / 450 g cherry tomatoes, on the vine

2 tbsp olive oil, plus extra to sprinkle

Salt and pepper

4 garlic cloves

1 cup / 35 g fresh cilantro (coriander) leaves

½ tsp paprika

½ tsp ground cumin

½ tsp curcuma (turmeric)

2 tbsp lemon juice

4 boneless chicken breasts, with skin on

Method

Prep and cook time: 1 hour

1 Preheat the oven to 180°C (350°F / Gas Mark 4).

2 Skin and cut the pumpkin into wedges, discarding the seeds, and put into an ovenproof dish with the tomatoes. Sprinkle with olive oil and season with salt and pepper.

3 Roughly chop the garlic. Put into a mortar with the cilantro (coriander) leaves, reserving a few to garnish, and the paprika, cumin, curcuma (turmeric), olive oil and lemon juice, and crush to a fine paste. Season with salt and pepper.

4 Rub the paste into the chicken breasts.

5 Place the chicken breasts on top of the vegetables, skin side up, and cook in the oven for about 30 minutes until golden brown and cooked through. Serve scattered with the reserved cilantro leaves.

CHICKEN AND MANGO SALAD

Ingredients

1 cucumber

2 scallions (spring onions)

3½ oz / 100 g bean sprouts

Salt and pepper

1 mango

4 cooked smoked boneless chicken breasts

6 tbsp shop-bought French dressing

3 tbsp sweet chili sauce

4 little gem lettuces

Method

Prep and cook time: 20 min

1 Cut the cucumber in half lengthways and then into slices. Shred the scallions (spring onions). Put the cucumber and scallions into a large bowl and add the bean sprouts. Season with salt and pepper.

2 Peel and slice the mango flesh either side of the stone, and then cut into thin slices.

3 Shred the chicken. Add the chicken and mango to the salad ingredients and mix together.

4 Pour the French dressing into a screw-top jar, add the sweet chili sauce and shake together. Toss the dressing into the salad.

5 Arrange the little lettuce leaves in the base of a large salad bowl. Spoon the salad on top and serve.

PAN-COOKED CHICKEN WITH RICE

Ingredients

1 cup / 200 g long grain rice

3½ cups / 900 ml vegetable broth (stock)

4 chicken legs, with skin on

Salt

2 green bell peppers

4 tomatoes

14 oz / 400 g frozen peas

2 tbsp paprika

1–2 tsp cayenne pepper

Method

Prep and cook time: 1 hour

1 Preheat the oven to 170°C (325°F / Gas Mark 3).

2 Wash and drain the rice. Put into a saucepan with 2½ cups / 600 ml of the vegetable broth (stock), bring to the boil and simmer for about 20 minutes until tender.

3 Season the chicken legs with salt, put into an ovenproof dish, and add the remaining vegetable broth. Cook the chicken in the oven for 20 minutes.

4 Meanwhile, roughly dice the green peppers, discarding the cores and seeds. Cut the tomatoes in half and dice the flesh, discarding the seeds. Add the peas, peppers and tomatoes to the rice and season with salt.

5 Remove the chicken legs from the baking dish. Put the rice and vegetables into the dish and mix with the meat juices. Place the chicken legs, skin side up, on top of the rice and sprinkle with paprika and cayenne pepper.

6 Return to the oven and cook for a further 15 minutes until the chicken legs are golden brown and cooked through.

CHICKEN AND MUSHROOM TAGLIATELLE

Ingredients

1 small onion

2 carrots

3 boneless chicken breasts, skinned

2 sprigs fresh thyme

1 cup / 225 ml water

2 tbsp dry sherry (optional)

Salt and pepper

1 lb / 450 g tagliatelle

9 oz / 250 g button mushrooms

2 garlic cloves

4 tbsp / 50 g butter

1 tbsp all-purpose (plain) white flour

Chopped fresh flat-leaf parsley,
to garnish

Method

Prep and cook time: 50 min

1 Cut the onion into quarters and the carrots into batons. Put in a large saucepan with the chicken, thyme, water and sherry, if using. Season generously with salt and pepper.

2 Bring to the boil, then reduce the heat and simmer for 15 minutes until the chicken is cooked through and tender when pierced with a fork. Add more water during cooking if necessary. Drain, set the chicken and vegetables aside and reserve the broth (stock).

3 Put the tagliatelle into a saucepan of boiling salted water and cook according to the packet instructions until tender but still with a slight bite.

4 Meanwhile, slice the mushrooms and crush the garlic. Melt the butter in a skillet (frying pan), add the mushrooms and garlic and fry for 5 minutes until softened.

5 Add the flour and cook for 1 minute. Gradually add the broth, stirring all the time, and cook until the sauce has thickened. Add the chicken and vegetables and heat through.

6 Drain the tagliatelle and divide between 4 serving plates. Put the chicken and mushroom mixture on top and serve sprinkled with parsley.

CHICKEN SATAY

Ingredients

1 red chili

1 shallot

2 garlic cloves

¼ tsp ground caraway

¼ tsp ground coriander

2 tbsp light soy sauce

4 tbsp coconut milk

2 tbsp vegetable oil

4 boneless chicken breasts, skinned

For the peanut sauce

5 oz / 150 g unsalted, shelled peanuts

¾ cup / 200 ml coconut milk

2 tbsp peanut butter

1 tsp curry powder

1 lemon

2–3 tsp brown sugar

3 tbsp whipping cream

Method

Prep and cook time: 1 hour plus 1 hour marinating

1 Finely chop the chili, discarding the seeds. Finely chop the shallot. Crush the garlic. Put all the vegetables in a large bowl.

2 Add the caraway, coriander, soy sauce, coconut milk and oil and mix together to make a marinade.

3 Slice the chicken breasts into ¾ inch (2 cm) wide strips. Add to the marinade and leave for at least 1 hour to marinate. Remove the chicken from the marinade and shake off any excess.

4 Thread the chicken strips on to wooden skewers so they make a wavy shape.

5 Heat the broiler (grill) and cook for about 10 minutes, turning and basting occasionally with the marinade, until cooked through.

6 To make the peanut sauce, toast the peanuts in a dry skillet (frying pan). Allow to cool and then crush finely in a mortar.

7 Put the coconut milk, crushed peanuts, peanut butter and curry powder in a saucepan and bring to the boil.

8 Remove a little of the zest from the lemon and squeeze out the juice. Mix the lemon zest and juice into the sauce. Season to taste with the sugar. Add the cream to the sauce and serve with the chicken skewers.

MEXICAN CHICKEN PANCAKES

Ingredients

Butter, for greasing

8 oz / 225 g cooked chicken

¼–½ tsp chili powder (optional)

1 bunch scallions (spring onions)

1¼ cups / 125 g all-purpose (plain) flour

2 eggs

Salt and pepper

⅔ cup / 200 ml milk

2 tbsp vegetable oil

⅔ cup / 200 ml sour (soured) cream

8 tbsp grated Cheddar cheese

Cilantro (coriander) leaves, to garnish

Method

Prep and cook time: 1 hour

1 Preheat the oven to 200°C (400°F / Gas Mark 6). Lightly butter 4 individual or 1 large ovenproof serving dish.

2 Cut the chicken into small pieces. Sprinkle the chicken with a little chili powder, if desired. Roughly chop the scallions (spring onions).

3 Put the flour and eggs into a large bowl and season with salt and pepper. Gradually beat in the milk to make a smooth batter.

4 Heat 1 tbsp of the oil in a skillet (frying pan). Add a ladleful of the batter and tip to cover the base of the pan. Cook for 1–2 minutes until the base is firm then flip and cook for a further 1 minute.

5 Repeat, using the remaining batter, to make 8 pancakes, interleaving the cooked pancakes with parchment paper.

6 Pour the sour cream into the base of the prepared dish or dishes. Sprinkle over the chopped scallions.

7 Place an eighth of the chicken pieces into the center of each pancake and add a little grated cheese to each, reserving a little to garnish.

8 Fold up each pancake, securing with a toothpick (cocktail stick), if needed. Carefully lift the pancakes on top of the sour cream mixture, allowing 2 per serving.

9 Bake in the oven for 15 minutes to warm through. Sprinkle the remaining cheese on top of each pancake and serve garnished with fresh cilantro (coriander) leaves.

CHICKEN IN BASIL SAUCE

Ingredients

1 lb / 450 g green ribbon noodles

4 oz / 120 g shallots

1 lb 8 oz / 675g boneless chicken breasts, skinned

1 lb 12 oz / 800 g tomatoes

1 cup / 25 g basil leaves

3 tbsp vegetable oil

Scant 1 cup / 200 g crème fraîche

7 tbsp whipping cream

Salt and pepper

½ cup / 50 g Parmesan cheese, half grated, half sliced

Method

Prep and cook time: 40 min

1 Cook the noodles according to the package directions until tender but still with a slight bite. Drain well.

2 Meanwhile, finely chop the shallots. Cut the chicken into cubes.

3 Blanch the tomatoes in boiling water, immerse in cold water and remove the skins. Coarsely chop the flesh.

4 Reserve a few of the basil leaves. Chop the rest into thin strips.

5 Heat the oil in a wok and fry the shallots until softened. Add the chicken and stir for about 1 minute.

6 Stir in the tomatoes, crème fraîche and cream. Add the basil and season with salt and pepper. Continue to fry over a high heat for 4 minutes, stirring continuously, until the chicken is cooked through.

7 Add the drained noodles and mix together. Garnish with slices of Parmesan cheese and the reserved basil leaves and serve the grated cheese separately for sprinkling on top.

SPICED CHICKEN WITH COUSCOUS

Ingredients

8 boneless chicken thighs

Salt and pepper

2 tsp medium curry powder

2 tsp paprika

½ tsp ground cinnamon

5 tbsp olive oil

1 onion

5 cloves garlic

1 cup / 150 g dried apricots

14 oz / 400 g canned tomatoes

2 cups / 375 g couscous

2 cups / 450 ml hot vegetable broth (stock)

4 tbsp / 50 g butter, diced

2 tbsp chopped parsley

4 tbsp toasted flaked almonds

Method

Prep and cook time: 45 min plus 30 min to marinate

1 Cut each chicken thighs into 3 pieces. Put into a large bowl and season generously with salt and pepper.

2 Add the curry powder, paprika, cinnamon and 3 tbsp oil and mix together. Spoon the mixture over the chicken and turn to coat all over. Cover and leave to marinate for 30 minutes.

3 Meanwhile dice the onion and the garlic. Chop the apricots.

4 Preheat the oven to 200°C (400°F / Gas Mark 6). Heat the remaining oil in a flameproof casserole dish. Add the chicken and cook over a medium heat for 10 minutes until browned all over. Add the chopped onion and garlic and cook for a further 2 minutes.

5 Add the tomatoes and apricots, bring to a boil then cover the dish and cook in the oven for 20 minutes until the chicken is cooked through.

6 Put the couscous into an ovenproof dish. Just before the chicken is cooked, pour in the hot broth (stock) and add 1 tsp salt. Stir and leave for 10 minutes until the broth has been absorbed.

7 Fluff up the couscous up with a fork. Dice the butter and dot over the couscous. Serve the spiced chicken, garnished with toasted flaked almonds, and accompany with the couscous.

CURRIED CHICKEN WITH COCONUT SAUCE

Ingredients

4 shallots

2 garlic cloves

4 boneless chicken breasts, skinned

2 small red chilies

9 oz / 250 g snow (sugar snap) peas

1 tbsp vegetable oil

¾ cup / 200 ml coconut milk

2 tbsp panang curry paste

2 tbsp fish sauce

2 tbsp sugar

Snipped chives, to garnish

Method
Prep and cook time: 30 min

1 Finely chop the shallots and garlic. Cut the chicken breasts into cubes. Finely chop 1 of the chilies, discarding the seeds. Slice the other into thin rings, discarding the seeds. Cut the snow (sugar snap) peas in half.

2 Heat the oil in a wok. Add the shallots and garlic and fry for 1 minute.

3 Add the coconut milk, stir in the curry paste and simmer over a low heat for 2 minutes.

4 Add the cubed chicken, fish sauce, sugar and finely chopped chili. Cook over a low heat for a further for 3 minutes.

5 Add snow peas and continue to stir and fry for 5 minutes until the chicken is cooked through. Serve garnished with the chili rings and chives.

COCONUT CHICKEN SOUP

Ingredients

2 boneless chicken breasts, skinned

8 oz / 225 g tofu

2 carrots

4 scallions (spring onions)

1 tbsp vegetable oil

1¾ cups / 400 ml coconut milk

1–2 tsp grated fresh ginger

2 cups / 475 ml water

4 oz / 115 g snow (sugar snap) peas

4 tbsp fish sauce

4 tbsp lime juice

Salt

Sugar

1 tbsp chopped fresh cilantro (coriander) leaves

Method
Prep and cook time: 35 min

1 Cut the chicken and tofu into cubes. Chop the carrots. Chop the white parts of the scallions (spring onions) and slice the green parts into long thin strips.

2 Heat the oil in a large saucepan. Add the carrots and chopped scallions and fry for 2–3 minutes.

3 Add the coconut milk, ginger and water and bring to the boil.

4 Add the chicken, tofu and snow (sugar snap) peas. Stir in the fish sauce and lime juice. Simmer for about 15 minutes, until the chicken is thoroughly cooked through.

5 Season with salt and sugar to taste. Stir in the cilantro (coriander) leaves.

6 Serve the soup garnished with the scallion strips.

KENTUCKY BURGOO SOUP

Ingredients

1 lb / 450 g chicken thighs, skinned

8 oz / 225 g stewing steak, cubed

3 cups / 750 ml chicken broth (stock)

3 tbsp tomato paste

¼ tsp cayenne pepper

Salt and pepper

3 small potatoes, roughly chopped

1 onion, sliced

14 oz / 400 g can chopped tomatoes

1 cup / 75 g fresh or frozen lima (butter) beans

1 tbsp Worcestershire sauce

½ cup / 125 ml water

14 oz / 400 g can sweetcorn kernels, drained

Method

Prep and cook time: 2 hours

1 Put the chicken, beef, broth (stock), tomato paste and cayenne pepper into a large saucepan. Season generously with salt and pepper. Simmer for 30 minutes.

2 Remove the chicken thighs from the pan and cut the meat away from the bones. Shred the chicken, discard the bones and return the chicken to the pan.

3 Add the potatoes, onions, tomatoes, lima (butter) beans and Worcestershire sauce. Cover the pan and simmer for 1 hour, stirring occasionally.

4 Add the water and sweetcorn, stirring to prevent it from scorching, and simmer for a further 20 minutes until the meat and vegetables are tender.

PERSIAN CHICKEN

Ingredients

1 cup / 200 g yellow split lentils

4 cups / 1 liter water

1 tsp salt

4 boneless chicken breasts, skinned

1 large onion

2 garlic cloves

1 carrot

1 stick celery

2 tbsp / 25 g butter

2 tsp garam masala

1 tsp curcuma (turmeric)

1 tsp hot chili powder

1 cup / 200 g canned
chopped tomatoes

Fresh spinach leaves, to garnish

Method

Prep and cook time: 1 hour 15 min

1 Put the lentils in a saucepan with the water and salt. Bring to the boil, then cover and simmer for 30 minutes until the lentils are tender and have absorbed most of the water.

2 Meanwhile, cut the chicken breasts into bite-size pieces. Chop the onion and crush the garlic. Slice the carrot and the celery.

3 Melt the butter in a large pan, add the onion, garlic, carrot and celery and cook for 3 minutes. Stir in the garam masala, curcuma (turmeric) and chilli powder to coat the vegetables then add the chicken and fry for 5 minutes.

4 Add the tomatoes and cooked lentils and a little more water if necessary. Cover and simmer gently for 15 minutes until the chicken is tender. Serve with spinach leaves and wholewheat noodles.

CHICKEN WITH PEPPER SAUCE

Ingredients

2 onions

1 garlic clove

3 red bell peppers

4 tbsp pitted (stoned) black olives

2 tbsp olive oil

2/3 cup / 150 ml vegetable broth (stock)

Salt and pepper

4 boneless chicken breasts, skinned

1 tbsp / 15 g butter

1 tbsp olive oil

1 lb / 450 g green tagliatelle

Method

Prep and cook time: 45 min

1 Chop the onion and garlic. Slice the red peppers into strips, discarding the cores and seeds. Slice the black olives.

2 Heat the oil in a large saucepan, add the onion and fry until translucent. Add the garlic and the red peppers. Fry for a further 3 minutes.

3 Pour in the vegetable broth (stock). Cover the pan and simmer for about 10 minutes. Using a hand-held blender, purée the sauce.

4 Return to the pan and simmer, uncovered, for about 5 minutes. Season to taste with salt and pepper.

5 Meanwhile, cut the chicken into thick slices and season with salt and pepper.

6 Heat the butter and olive oil in a large skillet (frying pan). Add the chicken pieces and fry for 3–4 minutes on each side until cooked through. Sprinkle generously with pepper.

7 Put the tagliatelle into a saucepan of boiling salted water and cook according to the packet instructions until tender but still with a slight bite.

8 Drain the tagliatelle and divide between 4 soup plates. Add the chicken with the sauce and serve sprinkled with the sliced olives, to garnish.

CHICKEN WITH LIME AND MINT

Ingredients

6 tbsp lime juice

1 tbsp fish sauce

2 tsp sugar

4 boneless chicken breasts, skinned

1 red chili

12 oz / 350 g rice noodles

Salt

1 carrot

1 small zucchini (courgette)

1 cup / 20 g fresh mint leaves

3 tbsp olive oil

Lime zest, to garnish

Method

Prep and cook time: 1 hour

1 Put 3 tbsp of the lime juice, the fish sauce and sugar in a bowl and mix together. Rub into the chicken breasts. Leave to marinate for about 30 minutes, turning from time to time. Meanwhile, finely chop the chili, discarding the seeds, and set aside.

2 Put the noodles into a saucepan of boiling salted water and cook according to the packet instructions until tender but still with a slight bite. Drain well, rinse under cold water and drain well again.

3 Cut the carrot and zucchini (courgette) lengthways and, using a mandolin vegetable slicer, cut into thin ribbons.

4 Put the noodles, carrot ribbons, zucchini ribbons and mint leaves in a large bowl. Mix 1 tbsp oil with the remaining lime juice. Add to the bowl and toss together. Put into serving bowls.

5 Heat the remaining oil in a skillet (frying pan). Remove the chicken from the marinade, add to the pan and fry for about 5 minutes on each side until tender and cooked through.

6 Thickly slice the chicken breasts widthways and arrange on top of the noodles. Sprinkle with the chopped chili and serve garnished with lime zest.

CHICKEN NOODLE SOUP

Ingredients

1 chicken, weighing about
3 lb 8 oz / 1.6 kg

1 inch / 2.5 cm piece fresh ginger

1 tbsp tomato paste

Salt and pepper

1 garlic clove

2 carrots

2 parsnips

1 celery stalk

1 onion

4 scallions (spring onions)

2 red chilies

3–4 oz / 100 g fine noodles

2 cups / 50 g fresh cilantro
(coriander) leaves

Method

Prep and cook time: 1 hour 20 min

1 Put the chicken in a large saucepan with enough cold water to cover. Bring to a boil and when the water boils, skim off any scum that rises to the surface.

2 Slice the ginger and add to the pan with the tomato paste, salt, pepper and garlic. Roughly chop the carrots, parsnips, celery and onion and add to the pan. Simmer over a low heat, partially covered, for about 45–60 minutes until the chicken is tender and cooked through.

3 Meanwhile, slice the scallions (spring onions) and finely chop the chilies, discarding the seeds. Set aside.

4 Remove the chicken from the pan. Strain the broth (stock) and return it to the pan, discarding the vegetables. Keep warm.

5 Put the noodles into a separate pan with some of the broth and cook according to the packet instructions until tender but still with a slight bite. Keep warm.

6 Remove the skin from the chicken, pull the meat from the bones and chop the meat into bite-size pieces.

7 To serve, put the meat and noodles into 4 serving bowls and sprinkle on the scallions and chopped chilies. Pour over the hot broth and garnish with the chopped cilantro (coriander).

CHICKEN PARMIGIANA

Ingredients

1 garlic clove

14 oz / 400 g can chopped tomatoes

1 tsp dried basil

1 tsp dried thyme

½ tsp sugar

Salt and pepper

8 thin chicken escalopes

1 lb / 450 g wholemeal spaghetti

2 eggs

¾ cup / 75 g grated Parmesan cheese

1½ cups / 85 g breadcrumbs

Vegetable oil, for shallow frying

7 oz / 200 g mozzarella cheese

Fresh basil, to garnish

Method

Prep and cook time: 50 min

1 To make the sauce, chop the garlic and put in a small saucepan with the tomatoes, dried basil, thyme and sugar. Bring to the boil then simmer for about 15 minutes, stirring occasionally.

2 Using a hand-held blender, blend the ingredients together to form a smooth purée. Season to taste with salt and pepper. Set aside.

3 Put the chicken escalopes between two sheets of plastic wrap (cling film) and beat with a meat mallet or rolling pin to flatten.

4 Cook the pasta in plenty of boiling, salted water according to the packet instructions.

5 Separate the eggs into 2 large bowls. Whisk the egg whites in a large bowl until stiff and then fold into the egg yolks with ½ cup / 50 g of the Parmesan cheese.

6 Spread the breadcrumbs on to a large plate. Dip the escalopes into the egg mixture and then into the breadcrumbs, coating both sides.

7 Meanwhile, preheat the broiler (grill). Heat the oil in a large skillet (frying pan) and fry the escalopes on both sides for about 3 minutes.

8 Place the escalopes on a heatproof dish, overlapping slightly in pairs. Slice the mozzarella cheese and lay on top of the escalopes. Put under the broiler for about 5 minutes.

9 When the spaghetti is cooked, drain and serve on to warmed serving plates. Put 2 escalopes on each plate and spoon over the sauce. Sprinkle with the remaining Parmesan cheese and serve immediately, garnished with fresh basil.

CHICKEN AND LEEK COBBLER

Ingredients

2 tbsp diced bacon

1 lb 8 oz / 650 g leeks

1 carrot

2 garlic cloves

2 large boneless chicken breasts, skinned

8 oz / 225 g ready-rolled puff pastry, thawed if frozen

Flour, for dusting

3 tbsp vegetable oil

5 tbsp dry white wine

2 cups / 475 ml chicken broth (stock)

Salt and pepper

Egg yolk, for glazing

Method

Prep and cook time: 45 min

1 Preheat the oven to 200°C (400°F / Gas Mark 6). Put the bacon in a skillet (frying pan) and fry in its own fat until browned. Leave to cool.

2 Meanwhile, thinly slice the leeks and carrot. Finely chop the garlic. Cut the chicken into bite-size pieces.

3 Sprinkle half the pastry sheets with the fried bacon and lay the other sheets on top. On a lightly floured surface, roll out to a thickness of ½ inch / 1 cm. Using a 2 inch / 5 cm cutter, cut out rounds.

4 Heat the oil in an ovenproof skillet and fry the garlic until softened. Add the chicken and brown on all sides. Add the leeks and carrot and fry for 1–2 minutes. Add the wine and cook until it has evaporated. Add the broth (stock) and season with salt and pepper.

5 Arrange the puff pastry rounds on top of the stew and brush with egg yolk.

6 Bake in the oven for 10–15 minutes until risen and golden brown.

COQ AU VIN

Ingredients

1 garlic clove

4 oz / 120 g thickly sliced bacon

4 tbsp all-purpose (plain) flour

Salt and pepper

1 chicken, cut into 4 pieces

¾ cup / 150 g butter

8 oz / 225 g shallots

8 oz / 225 g chestnut mushrooms

1 bottle dry white wine

3 sprigs fresh thyme plus some
for garnish

For the beurre manié

1 oz / 2 tbsp / 25 g butter

¼ cup / 25 g all-purpose (plain) flour

Method

Prep and cook time: 1 hour

1 Preheat the oven to 180°C (350°F / Gas Mark 4).
Crush the garlic. Dice the bacon.

2 Put the flour into a large shallow dish and season
generously with salt and pepper. Dip the chicken
portions in the flour to coat.

3 Melt the butter in a large flameproof casserole
dish. When foaming, add the chicken portions and
fry until browned all over, turning as needed.

4 Add the shallots, garlic and diced bacon and fry
until golden brown. Stir in the mushrooms. Pour in
the wine and add the thyme. Bring to the boil then
cover the casserole.

5 Cook in the oven for 40 minutes until the chicken
and vegetables are tender.

6 Put the butter and flour for the beurre manié in
a small bowl and mix together. Return the coq au
vin to the hob and cook over a medium heat. Stir in
the beurre manié, a small piece at a time, until the
sauce thickens slightly and is glossy. Serve garnished
with fresh thyme.

CHICKEN AND NECTARINE SKEWERS

Ingredients

4 boneless chicken breasts, skinned

3 nectarines

3 scallions (spring onions)

2 tbsp olive oil

Salt and pepper

4 tbsp runny honey

Baby spinach leaves, to garnish

Method

Prep and cook time: 30 min

1 Cut the chicken into bite-size pieces. Cut the nectarines in half, remove the pits (stones) and cut the flesh into wedges. Slice the scallions (spring onions) diagonally, into 4 cm / 1½ inch pieces.

2 Thread the chicken pieces, nectarines and scallions on to wooden skewers. Brush with the oil and season with salt and pepper.

3 Preheat the broiler (grill). Cook the kebabs, turning frequently, for 6–8 minutes or until the chicken is cooked through. Baste with the honey during the last few minutes of the cooking time.

4 Arrange the leaves on serving plates and place the kebabs on top to serve.

PIRI PIRI CHICKEN

Ingredients

4 fresh red chilies

½ cup / 100 ml olive oil

2 garlic cloves

1 tsp dried oregano

2 tsp paprika

¼ cup / 50 ml red wine vinegar

Salt and pepper

4 boneless chicken breasts, with skin on

1 red bell pepper

1 yellow bell pepper

1 tbsp chopped fresh parsley, to garnish

Method

Prep and cook time: 1 hour plus 1 hour marinating

1 Preheat the oven to 190°C (375°F / Gas Mark 5). Put the chilies in a roasting pan with a little of the oil and roast in the oven for 10 minutes. Leave to cool. Meanwhile, finely chop the garlic.

2 Roughly chop the cooled chilies, discarding the seeds. Put the chilies, garlic, oregano, paprika, olive oil and vinegar in a saucepan, and simmer for 2–3 minutes. Season with salt.

3 Using a hand-held blender or mini food processor, blend the mixture to form a purée.

4 Put the chicken, in a single layer, in a shallow dish and spread half the piri piri sauce evenly over the chicken. Cover and leave to marinate for 1 hour.

5 Increase the oven temperature to 200°C (400°F / Gas Mark 6). Preheat a large ridged skillet or griddle pan on the hob. Season the marinated chicken with pepper and cook, skin side down, on the pan for 2–3 minutes until golden brown. Turn and cook for a further 2 minutes.

6 Transfer the griddled chicken to a roasting pan and roast in the oven for 30 minutes or until cooked through, basting regularly with the remaining piri piri sauce. (Any remaining piri piri sauce can be kept in a screw-top jar, in the refrigerator, for about 1 month.)

7 Meanwhile, cut the red and yellow peppers into chunky pieces, discarding the cores and seeds. Thread the pieces on to 4 bamboo skewers and griddle for 10 minutes.

8 To serve, slice the chicken and accompany with the griddled peppers and tomato salsa and boiled rice, if wished. Sprinkle over chopped parsley to garnish.

CHINESE-STYLE CHICKEN

Ingredients

2 red bell peppers

7 oz / 200 g can bamboo shoots

4 scallions (spring onions)

4 boneless chicken breasts, skinned

4 tbsp vegetable oil

5 tbsp soy sauce

1 tbsp corn starch (cornflour)

Salt and pepper

1/3 cup / 50 g cashew nuts

1½ cups / 150 g bean sprouts

2 tbsp oyster sauce

Method

Prep and cook time: 25 min

1 Slice the red peppers into fine strips, discarding the cores and seeds. Roughly chop the bamboo shoots. Roughly chop the scallions (spring onions). Slice the chicken breasts into thick strips.

2 Heat the oil in a wok or large skillet (frying pan), add the chicken and stir-fry for 4 minutes. Remove from the pan and set aside.

3 Add the peppers, bamboo shoots and scallions and stir-fry for 3 minutes.

4 Mix the soy sauce with the corn starch (cornflour) and add a little water to make a smooth paste. Stir into the vegetables.

5 Return the chicken to the pan and season with salt and pepper.

6 Stir in the cashew nuts and bean sprouts, heat briefly, check the chicken is cooked through, and season to taste with the oyster sauce. Serve in bowls.

ROAST CHICKEN WITH PORK, ONION AND SAGE STUFFING

Ingredients

1 medium chicken, trussed

6 oz / 150 g ground pork

1 cup / 50 g fresh breadcrumbs

1 small onion, finely chopped

2 tsp dried sage

Salt and pepper

1 stick / 100 g butter

Parsley, to garnish

For the vegetables:

1½ lb / 600 g small new potatoes, washed

3 tbsp olive oil

1 lb / 400 g carrots, cut into batons

8 oz / 200 g green beans, trimmed

½ stick / 50 g butter, melted

Method

Prep and cook time: 2 hours

1 Heat the oven to 375°F (190°C / Gas mark 5).

2 Mix the pork, breadcrumbs, onion and sage, season with salt and pepper and stuff into the cavity of the chicken.

3 Smear the chicken with the butter, sprinkle with salt and place in a roasting pan.

4 Roast the chicken for about 1¾ hours, basting with the juices every 20 minutes or so. The chicken is cooked when a skewer is inserted into the thickest part of the thigh and the juices run clear. Rest the chicken for 15 minutes in a warm place before serving.

5 While the chicken is cooking, put the potatoes in a large pan of salted water and bring to a boil. Simmer for about 15 minutes or until the potatoes are just tender. Heat the oil in a skillet and sauté the potatoes until golden brown. Set aside and keep warm.

6 While the chicken is resting, steam or boil the carrots and green beans until tender. Drain well and coat with the melted butter. Serve the chicken and the vegetables sprinkled with chopped parsley.

Published by Transatlantic Press

First published in 2011

Transatlantic Press
38 Copthorne Road, Croxley Green, Hertfordshire WD3 4AQ

© Transatlantic Press

Images and Recipes by StockFood © The Food Image Agency

Recipes selected by Jonnie Léger, StockFood

A catalogue record for this book is available from the British Library.

ISBN 978-907176-42-5

Printed in China